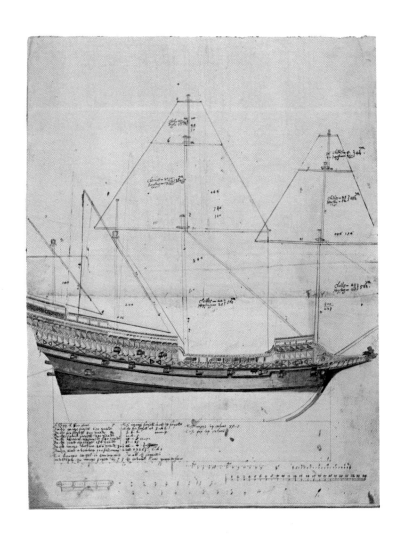

I

Distribution in the United States of America by
Mine Publications, Inc.,
25 Groveland Terrace,
Minneapolis, Minnesota 55403.

Published simultaneously in Great Britain by
Blond Educational Ltd.,
Iliffe House, Oadby, Leicestershire,
England.

Printed in Canada.
1   2   3   4   5   76   75   74   73   72

Themes in Art *provides a fresh approach to the study of fine art. Each book is based on a theme or subject, rather than on a stylistic or historical era. Intended for intermediate students,* Sailing Ships *is an introduction to the study of design as it is seen in the historical development of ships and nautical instruments.*

Cover:

Unknown Venetian Painter
The Battle of Lepanto
(*1571, Oil painting, 50" x 91½"*)
National Maritime Museum, Greenwich.

Page i:

Drawing
Elizabethan Galleon
(*from Samuel Pepys' collection, "Fragments of Ancient English Shipwrightery"*)
The Master and Fellows of Magdalen College, Cambridge.

Sailing Ships

George Wallace, M.A.
Associate Professor of Fine Art
McMaster University, Hamilton, Ontario

Holt, Rinehart and Winston of Canada, Limited
Toronto   Montreal

Distributed in the United States of America by
Mine Publications, Inc.

Introduction

For nine years of my life I lived in a busy seaport in the west of England. On fine days, old men would stroll along the quays or just sit in the sun and watch the ships and small boats that constantly moved about the harbour or came in to be refitted in the dockyard. I can remember the excitement of the people of Falmouth when one of the last of the Australian wheat ships, the four-masted sailing ship "Pamir," anchored in the bay on her way up channel. Many of the old men could remember when the harbour had been crowded with sailing ships. These old seamen looked at ships with an affectionate yet critical eye, because they knew from experience that each ship has distinct individual characteristics that give it a "personality" of its own. For instance, some ships are calm-weather boats, others handle well in heavy seas; some are easy to load, others are not.

All seamen have had to meet the unpredictable dangers of the sea and their lives have depended on how well their ships have worked in desperate circumstances, so it is hardly surprising that they have had very strong feelings of like or dislike for individual ships. These

Pieter Brueghel the Elder (c. 1525-69, Flemish)
Landscape with the Fall of Icarus
(c. 1555, Oil painting on panel now transferred to canvas, 29" x 44⅛")
This strange and beautiful landscape painting, where the supposed subject of the picture, the death of Icarus, happens almost unnoticed in a corner, is dominated by the most accomplished 16th century painting of a ship. Like several of the 16th century ships illustrated here, Brueghel's vessel has four masts, with the fore and main masts carrying huge square sails.
Musées Royaux des Beaux-Arts de Belgique, Bruxelles.

strong feelings made them look at the design and proportions of a boat very closely and from its appearance to make expert judgments of how it could be expected to work. For some sailors their feelings seem to have gone further, they thought of ships in the way many people think of paintings or sculptures, they thought of them as being beautiful. When they spoke of a "pretty ship" they were assessing many qualities of shape and arrangement and whether these seemed "right." By these judgments they implied that a ship that looked well would also sail well.

Other people also have considered the possibility of a connection between efficiency and beauty. Some utilitarian things such as scientific instruments or farm machinery often have simple, uncluttered shapes similar to those in modern sculpture. Whether there is a relationship between the look of a machine and how well it works is an interesting question and one which has intrigued architects and designers over the past sixty or seventy years. Some architects have stood the idea on its head by arguing that if a building works perfectly it must be beautiful. This theory, called "functionalism," begs the question rather than giving an answer. The development of sailing ships constantly confronts us with this question of the possibility of a relation between function and beauty. For sailing ships not only play a very important part in the history of the Western world and evolve through more than three thousand years, a longer history than for any equally complicated piece of machinery, but they have been considered to be beautiful as perhaps no other utilitarian object has been.

There are other qualities to be found in the study of these old ships. While we seem often to think of machinery as something to be used up and thrown away, these shipbuilders, like other craftsmen, seem to have thought of the ships they made not merely as products of their skill but as an expression of their personalities and a justification of their worth as men. For example, Elizabethan shipbuilders gave their ships graceful lines like a fish so that they too should move easily through the water. However, they did not think of their ships as merely efficient machines and nothing else; the pride that shipbuilders and captains took in their ships was reflected in the care with which they maintained them, in the colours which they chose to paint them, and particularly in the gorgeous decorations with which they often embellished them. These decorations on the bow and stern of warships and merchantmen were never allowed to interefere with their efficiency, and shipbuilders did not change the design of their ships merely to make last year's ship look out-of-date, but only to improve the new ship in some way so that it could carry more cargo or larger guns; or to make it sail faster or closer to the wind. In this characteristic these designers seem more serious than many of ours today, for though they may sometimes build with ostentatious magnificence, they also seem more honestly concerned with quality. These old ships survive for us only in pictures and models, having long ago been wrecked, broken up for firewood or left to rot in muddy estuaries; but their design teaches us something of the dignity of things well made. In a society such as ours, in which more and more things are shoddy and expendable, well-made things whatever they are, establish a standard by which we can measure our own worth.

Hans Holbein the Younger (1497-1543, Swiss)
The Sailboat
(*Drawing, c. 1535.*)
Though this is a workman-like small ship, it is very much a "Ship of Fools", for the crew seem to be concentrating their attention on anything but sailing. Stadelsches Kunstinstitut, Frankfurt.

4

Ships in Ancient Times

Although no ships survive from the great early seagoing nations of the Mediterranean, Egypt, Phoenecia and Greece, we know something of their shape and rigging from pictures on coins, from decorations on pots and from terra cotta and carved sculptures. In general, these ships seem to have been of two kinds, oared galleys and trading ships with sails. The galleys seem to have been used as warships. They were narrow, low and up to 150 feet long. However, a ship of that length was only 16 feet wide, with a shallow draught of about four feet. Steered by two rudder paddles attached to the sides of the boat near the stern, they were very manoeuverable, for the usual way to attack was to drive a pointed metal ram on the bow into the side of the enemy ship. Though they were chiefly propelled by oars, they carried a single square sail on a removable mast in the centre of the ship. These specialized fighting ships were fast over short stretches of calm sea, but, because of their large crews and shallow *draught*, they were not economical as cargo carriers. Sailing boats with much wider and deeper hulls were used for that purpose.

Greek Vase Painting
Odysseos and the Sirens
(late 6th century B.C.)
Attic red figure stamnos (a two-handled, full bellied jar used to store wine and other supplies) from Vulci. In this painting you can see the ram bow and two steering paddles characteristic of Greek warships. British Museum, London.

Ancient Egyptian Wall Relief
Egyptian Ship
(early 15th century B.C., about 20" high)
Detail from a carved and painted wall decoration of the Temple of Queen Hatshepsut at Dier-el Bekari near Luxor Egypt showing one of several boats that made the expedition to the land of Punt.

This is a large ship about seventy feet long rowed by oarsmen, but it also has a single mast with a large square sail. It was steered, as were all early ships, by two steering paddles lashed to the side of the ship near the stern.

Royal Ontario Museum, Toronto.

We have fewer pictures of these merchant ships than we have of the galleys. They seem to have been raised much higher out of the water, that is, they had more *freeboard* so that waves could not break over the sides, and they had one large square sail. As they used oars only to get in and out of harbour, they needed a small crew and were therefore inexpensive to work. A boat with this kind of sail works well in *a following wind* but is inefficient when sailing *across or into the wind*. Such a ship would have to wait for a favourable wind to travel in the right direction, rather than *working up wind* by *tacking*. Also, the two side rudders were difficult to handle when sailing across the wind, for as the boat leaned over one paddle would be almost out of the water while the other would be so deeply submerged as to be almost unmanageable.

The Romans improved the sailing qualities of earlier merchant ships by adding a small sail, the artemon, on a bowsprit. Because it was set in front of the bow, this sail could be used as a wind rudder to turn the ship when it was moving slowly.

We know very few details about Greco-Roman ships, but we do know that similar kinds of vessels, both cargo boats and galleys, were used in the Mediterranean long after the fall of the Roman Empire.

Though there are great storms in the Mediterranean Sea, it is generally less stormy and changeable than the seas along the Atlantic coasts of Europe and it has weaker and less variable tides. Ships designed to work in the dangerous and unpredictable waters of the Atlantic were different from those used in the Mediterranean.

Assyrian relief from the Palace of Sennachereb at Kouyunjik.

A Phoenician Warship

Like Greek and Roman galleys, this ship is rowed by two tiers of oarsmen and has a pointed ram (projecting from the bow) used to sink enemy ships. It has an upper deck with what appears to be matting bulwarks, behind which archers and spearmen stand.

British Museum, London.

Greek Bronze Fibula

Two Archers, a Ship and Three Fish

(late 8th century, 8½″ high).

This engraved decoration shows some of the characteristic features of Greek ships; namely, the high curved stern post, the steering paddle with its tiller-like handle and the ram projecting at the bow. There also seem to be additional spikes at the bow and stern.

National Museum, Athens. Photo by courtesy of the German Archaeological Institute, Athens.

Phoenecian Coin
Coin from Sidon
This coin shows a ship very similar in design to a
Greek galley.
British Museum, London.

Greek Vase Painting
Attic Black Figure Cup.
The decoration on this cup shows the difference between a Greek merchant ship on the left and a bireme, or two-tiered galley, on the right. The merchant ship has no ram on the bow and has much higher sides. It would also have been wider and of deeper draught.
British Museum, London.

Roman Carved Frieze
Ships Approaching a Lighthouse
(*Found at Ostia, the Roman port at the mouth of the Tiber, this was probably made about 200 A.D.*)
Though the three merchant ships shown here are not at the right scale, you can see some of the features of these large, sturdy vessels which were capable of carrying 120 to 250 tons of cargo. Many of them were used to carry corn from Egypt to Italy. They used large oars or sweeps only to manoeuvre in the harbour. Otherwise they depended on a single large square sail and the artemon, the small sail set on a bowsprit.
Photo by courtesy of the Ny Carlsberg Glyptotek, Copenhagen.

Greek Vase Painting
Two Ships under Sail
Attic black figure wine cup, signed Nikosthenes. This painting shows the high curving sterns of Greek ships. The ladder-like frames tied to these sterns are thought to be gangplanks for boarding.
Louvre, Paris, Photo des Musées Nationaux.

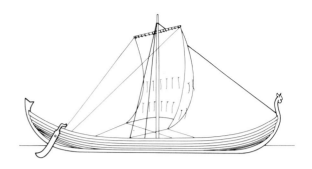

Medieval Ships

We know in detail the shape, construction and decoration of the ships used by the Vikings in their exploration along the coasts of Europe and across the North Atlantic. Two well-preserved examples of these ships have been found in burial sites in Norway. Both are beautiful, with graceful, curving lines and they differ in two important ways from the ships that were used in the Mediterranean. The Viking ships had a high curving peak at both the bow and stern, so that as long as they were headed into the waves they would not swamp easily. Greek and Roman ships seem to have been "carvel built" (the planks were fitted edge to edge and nailed to the ribs); by contrast Viking ships were "clinker" or "clincher built," with each plank partly overlapping the one below and riveted together, as well as being nailed to the ribs. These two features made these ships into wonderfully strong and seaworthy vessels, able to survive the harsh North Atlantic weather and travel great distances, from Labrador and Iceland to the coasts of France and Spain and even into the Mediterranean.

The Oseberg Ship

Carved Prow
(*c. 800 A.D.*)
Universitetets Oldsaksamling, *Oslo, Norway*.

13

The Normans were descendants of Vikings who had settled in Northern France and the ships used by William the Conqueror for his attack on England shown in the Bayeaux tapestry (p. 18) are similar to the Oslo ships. They have the same high stern decorated with carving, the same kind of rudder and the same central mast and square sail. One ship in the Bayeaux tapestry even has the same number of oars (sixteen to a side) and was presumably much the same size as the Gokstad ship, made two hundred years earlier.

Except for the addition of fighting castles to the bow and stern from which archers could defend the ship, very few changes appear in the design of northern ships for almost three hundred years. However these "castles" were important, for although at first they appeared to be temporary structures and only later were they altered to fit the shape of the hull, modified "castles" remain as a part of most ships until about 1800. The *forecastle* or fo'c'sle, was used as a fighting castle for some time until it became the crew's quarters. The aftercastle, or summercastle, was used to make cabins for "important people" and later became the officers' quarters and staterooms.

The ship on the Seal of Ipswich (p. 17) shows one very important improvement. It has a rudder hinged to the sternpost. Such a rudder not only made steering much easier, but was also less likely to be damaged by heavy seas than the earlier steering paddle lashed to the side of the ship.

The little painting of Venice (p. 21) is interesting for many reasons. It is a lively picture of a busy, prosperous city divided by canals on which are several buildings still to be seen today. It also shows, moored in the lagoon, three ships which some fine gentlemen are about to board. Two of the ships are clinker built, single masted, and have castles *fore* and *aft*. The third ship has two smaller masts and banks of oars. It is a galley not so very different from the warships of ancient Greece or from those that the Turks and Venetians used at the great sea battle of Lepanto, shown on the cover of this book, which took place about two hundred and seventy years after this picture was made. On the cover, you can see Venetian and Ottoman galleys, long shallow boats with a metal ram projecting from the bow, which are very similar to Greek galleys two thousand years earlier.

A distinctive Mediterranean tradition of shipbuilding survived through the Middle Ages. This tradition and that of the Atlantic coasts influence one another and both are gradually changed by the introduction of new ideas. At first improvements happen very gradually, but from 1450 onwards there is a great and an increasingly rapid improvement in ship design.

Viking Ship
The Gokstad Ship
(*c. 850-900 A.D. Made of oak, this ship weighed about 20 tons and is 79 ft. long, 16¾ ft. wide and 6¾ ft. deep amidships.*)
This, the best preserved of Viking ships, had been used as the burial place of a man thought to be Olav Geirstadalv. A grave chamber of wood had been built on the deck of the ship containing the body of the dead man and a collection of his domestic goods and treasure. The ship and all it contained was then buried under a mound of earth.

Rowed by 32 oars (16 to a side) and with a square sail on a centre mast, this very seaworthy ship was made more sturdy by having a full deck from bow to stern supported on crossbeams. You can see the steering paddle and tiller at the stern.

Found in the same grave were three small row-boats from 21 to 33 feet long which are very like Newfoundland dories in design.
Universitetets Oldsaksamling, Oslo, Norway.

Viking Ship
The Oseberg Ship
(c. 800 A.D. Made of oak, this ship is 70½ ft. long, 16¾ ft. wide and 5 ft. deep amidships.)
Less seaworthy than the Gokstad ship, this vessel may have been used as a pleasure ship in sheltered waters. Its construction is similar to the Gokstad find but it is very richly decorated. You can see the oar ports (30 in all) along the sides. The oars are stacked in fork-like racks on either side of the ship where they were stored when the ship was under sail.

This wonderful discovery contained the bodies of two women, thought to be Queen Asa and her maid-servant, and an extraordinarily rich collection of personal and domestic treasures. Among these were three sleighs and a wagon all decorated with entwined designs which had once been brightly painted, similar to those on the bow and stern posts of the ship.
Universitetets Oldsaksamling, Oslo, Norway.

The Seal of Ipswich
Ships at Sea
(*13th century, 2⅞" diameter*)
Like most mediaeval merchant ships of the Atlantic coasts, the vessel shown here is short and broad and stands high out of the water. Its bulging hull could carry a large cargo and its high sides ("large freeboard") make it less likely to be swamped by heavy seas. Two other changes distinguish it from Viking or Norman ships. It has two fighting castles in the bow and stern and the steering paddle has been replaced by a rudder hinged onto the stern post.
British Museum, London.

Carved Misericord
Two Boat Builders
(*14th century*)
A misericord is a small ledge fixed to the underside of choir stalls. When the monk stood and folded up his stall seat he could lean against this ledge and in fact sit when he seemed to stand. "Misericordia" means "pity" in Latin. The little seat took pity on him! They are generally decorated with grotesque or humourous carvings. This oak carving gives a good idea of the rounded, bulging, clinker built hull of a mediaeval ship.
Reproduced by courtesy of the Dean and Chapter of St. Davids Cathedral, Pembrokeshire, Wales.

following page:

Bayeux Tapestry
Tenture de la Reine Mathilde
(*c. 1073-1088, wool embroidery on linen, detail showing Norman ships sailing towards England.*)
Probably the hulls, decorated prows and the shields hung on the gunnels of Viking ships were painted similarly bright colours.
Avec authorisation spéciale de la ville de Bayeux.

St. Nicholas Chapel, King's Lynn
Decorated Stall End
(14th century, carved oak.)
Gradually the rigging of sailing ships became more complex as the number of masts increased and new sail designs developed. The ship illustrated here has two masts. The stern or mizzenmast has a triangular lateen sail which was to be used on almost all large ships for the next 400 years.
Victoria and Albert Museum, London.

Gothic Miniature
A View of Venice
(c. 1400)
This delightful miniature is from "Les Livres du Graunt Caam."
The Bodleian Library, Oxford University.

Detail of A View of Venice *showing the two sailing ships and an oared galley in the foreground.*

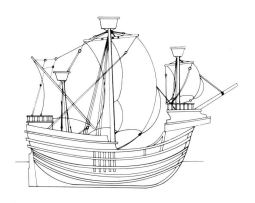

Ships of the European Expansion

During the fifteenth, sixteenth and seventeenth centuries trade and exploration developed and the European nations, first Portugal and Spain and later England, Holland and France expanded their mercantile empires around the world. This growth was made possible by the development of ships and of the art of navigation. Successful exploration, trading and naval warfare were all very closely connected, necessitating constant improvement in ship design and innovations in navigational skills. So it is not surprising to find a great increase in the number of sailing ships in use and also in the size, speed, armament and general efficiency of these vessels. These improvements were of two kinds: improvements in the design of hulls and improvements in the design of masts and sails. Of course both of these changes affected one another.

The ships of the Middle Ages were broad in relation to their length. The ship on the Ipswich Seal is sturdily built with a great deal of freeboard so that it could carry a large cargo without becoming swamped in heavy seas. However, during the fifteenth and sixteenth centuries the part of the ship below the water

Gothic Miniature
Jonah Thrown Overboard
(*late 15th century, from the "Diurnal" of René de Lorraine*)
Though these pictures and carvings suggest some of the characteristics of mediaeval ships, none of these ships have survived so that we have no accurate knowledge of them, as we do of Viking ships.
Bibliothèque Nationale, Paris.

line gradually became more streamlined as ships became longer in relation to their width. Since it was more important for a merchant ship to carry a large cargo than to sail very fast, they were usually broadly built with spacious holds. There was a period in the nineteenth century when it became important to ship certain cargos, particularily tea and wool, to market quickly, and fast sailing clippers were designed to do this. Such famous clipper ships as the "Lightening" and the "Cutty Sark" are the climax to the design of merchant sailing ships.

Warships, on the other hand, were designed to do more than sail fast and manoeuver easily; they had to make a firm platform from which large cannons could be fired. At first cannons were so small and inefficient that they could do little damage to enemy ships. Mounted on swivels on the sides of the fore and aft castles, they were fired at the enemy crew. When cannons were designed large enough to make holes in other ships, they were so heavy that if they were not placed near the water line, they would have capsized the ship when they were fired. This meant that gunports had to be cut in the sides of the ship and closed with wooden shutters so that the waves would not break through in stormy weather. The muzzles of the guns were pushed out of these *gunports* to fire. At first the cutting of these holes through the side of the ship was difficult to do without dangerously weakening the whole hull. However once that was solved, warships were built to carry one, two and three tiers of guns arranged so that the big guns were near the water line and the smaller ones above. Large warships had as many as one hundred guns, a few firing fore and aft but most of them firing as *broadsides*.

To obtain sufficient power for increasingly heavy ships the number and kind of sails that could be set became increasingly important. In the miniature of Jonah being thrown to the whale, the ship has three masts instead of one. This change in rigging made European ships more efficient. The older one-masted square-sailed ships were dependent on favourable winds and were most efficient when they used their sails like kites to pull them along before the wind. These new sail designs made it easier to tack into the wind, that is to sail a series of diagonal zigzags towards the wind. The two- and three-masted ships used a triangular sail, called a lateen, on at least one of their masts. This design of sail is an improvement that European sailors learned from the Arabs. Square sails were set on *yards* rigged across the ship, whereas lateen sails were set fore and aft like the sails on a modern yacht. Present-day Arab *dhows* use two lateen sails, but European ships generally had square sails on the fore and main masts and a lateen on the *mizzenmast*. This sail plan was introduced on the Atlantic coast during the fifteenth century and, although gradually improved, was essentially the same even in the nineteenth century. Perhaps more than anything else, these new sails made possible the great Portuguese and Spanish explorations to the East and West Indies.

In the fifteenth century, ships had two, three and four masts. However, from the time of Queen Elizabeth improved design of sails enabled a three-masted ship to be as efficient while being much easier to operate than one with four masts.

In the seventeenth and eighteenth centuries masts were made taller and the huge square sails of the beginning of the sixteenth century, which must have been very heavy to raise and *trim*, were replaced by several smaller square sails with horizontal rows of *reef points* arranged at intervals so that part of the sail could be folded up on itself and tied. In this way sails could be reefed, that is, reduced in size or completely folded away close to the *yard-arms*, when the wind became too strong.

In the sixteenth century the bowsprit was chiefly used to brace the masts and had only one sail, the sprit sail (a small square sail on a yard beneath the bowsprit). In the next century large ships had this sail rigged on a sprit sail topmast, a small precarious mast sticking up at the end of the bowsprit. Later still this sail was replaced by more useful jib sails, triangular sails set between the foremast and the bowsprit.

The pressure of the wind against the sails made it necessary for the mast to be firmly braced into the hull. To support the mast, Roman and Viking ships had two mainstays, one to the bow and one to the stern. As masts were made taller and more sails were set, more stays were needed. When sails such as lateens and jibs were introduced, allowing ships to sail across the wind, the rigging from the mast to the side of the ship became very important. Part of this side rigging, "the shrouds," was used as rope ladders so that the crew could climb to the "tops" (the small platforms halfway up the mast) and out on to the yard-arms to adjust the sails. At least four ropes were needed to raise and trim each sail; some used more. This constantly redesigned power system is one of the attractive parts of sailing ships, in both the shapes of their full bulging sails and in the pattern of lines made by their masts and rigging.

Model
"Santa Maria"
(1492)

Though we have little accurate information about Columbus' ship, this model made in 1892 would seem to be inaccurate in some details, for the original almost certainly had a round stern. The "Santa Maria" was about 95 feet long and 26½ feet in beam. The model shows clearly the difference between the square sails on the fore and main masts which are similar to those on Greek or Viking ships and the triangular lateen sail set fore and aft on the mizzenmast.

British Crown copyright, Science Museum, London.

Model

A Portuguese Caravela

(c. 1535)

During the 16th century the size of ships increased and four-masted vessels were designed. This model is of an unusually large ship used by the Emperor Charles V to capture Tunis in 1535. It was about 114 feet long and of 400 tons burden. It was rigged with four lateen sails and with square sails only on the foremast. This design is characteristic of the Mediterranean. However, these large lateen sails were heavy to handle and needed almost twice as large a crew as for square sails of similar size. On the Atlantic coasts the mainmast was almost always rigged with square sails. The rigging of these ships could be changed fairly easily. During his first voyage Columbus altered one of his small ships, the "Nina," from lateen to square rig during a week's stay in the Canary Islands.

British Crown Copyright, Science Museum, London.

Flemish Woodcut
Portuguese attack on Aden in 1513
(1514)
*This print gives an idea of the ships used in explora-
tion around the Cape and into the Indian Ocean.*
British Museum, London.

Jacopo de Barbari (c. 1450-1511, *Venetian*)
Plan of Venice
(1500, Woodcut in six parts, the detail shown here is part of the lower right-hand block, 27" x 18".)
The ships shown at anchor in this print have the rounded deep hulls characteristic of merchant ships. Several also have the sloping spars used for lateen sails.
British Museum, London.

Cornelus Anthonizoon
Portuguese Carracks off a Rocky Coast
(c. 1520-30, Oil painting, 31" x 57")
The scene is dominated by a splendid high castled carrack of the kind used by the Portuguese for the East Indies trade. The mainsail shows several innovations. By attaching it to the mast and to additional halyards, the great sail is divided into several pockets. Such large sails were heavy to handle so that the general development of sail design over the next centuries tended towards an increase in number and versatility of sails rather than an increase in their size. You can see how ships sailing on different tacks could set their sails to catch the wind.
National Maritime Museum, Greenwich.

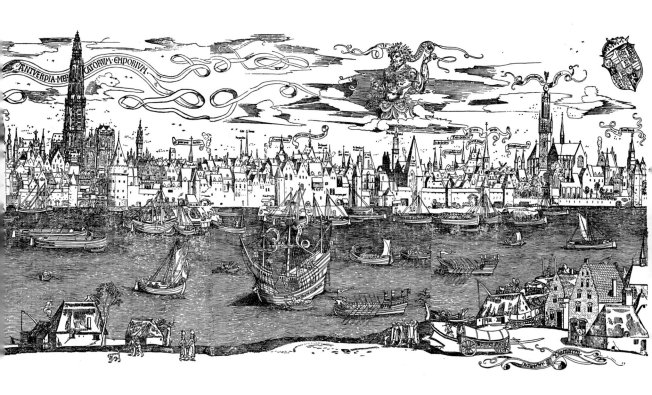

Flemish
View of Antwerp Harbour
(*1515, woodcut*)
Cabinet des Estamps, Antwerp.

Unknown Venetian Painter
The Battle of Lepanto
(*1571, Oil painting, 50″ x 91½″*)
National Maritime Museum, Greenwich.

Drawing

Elizabethan Galleon

(*from Samuel Pepys' collection, "Fragments of Ancient English Shipwrightery"*)

This drawing and the one on p. i are two of a series of drawings believed to have been made by the Elizabethan shipwright Matthew Baker about 1586. This one compares the shape of a fish with that of the hull of a boat and shows that Baker was concerned that his ships should have clean, streamlined lines under water.

The other drawing shows not only the shape of the hull and upper works but also the arrangement of the masts. These drawings are important because they give authentic contemporary information about the painting and decoration of Elizabethan ships. The hulls were "paid" with a mixture of linseed oil, resin and turpentine but the upper works were painted in geometrical patterns of strongly contrasting colours.

The Master and Fellows of Magdalen College, Cambridge.

Model
An Elizabethan Galleon
(*c. 1600*)
*As you can see this model is made from Baker's
drawing on p.i. Ten of the larger ships in the English
fleet that destroyed the Armada would have been
four-masters similar to this. Most of the remaining
ships were small three-masters with only one lateen
sail each.*
British Crown Copyright, Science Museum, London.

A modern conjectural model
"Mayflower"
(1620)
By contrast with the "Royal Prince," the "May-
flower" (in which the Pilgrim Fathers sailed to
New England) was a small merchant ship of about
180 tons.
British Crown Copyright, Science Museum, London.

Hendrick Cornelisz Vroom
The Arrival at Flushing in May 1613 of Frederick V, Elector Palatine with his Consort Elisabeth, Daughter of James I of England.
(1623, oil painting)

The large ship near the centre of the picture is the "Royal Prince" of 1610. It is very similar to Elizabethan ships in general design but the style of decoration has changed. The painted designs of the previous reign have been replaced by elaborate gilded carvings. During the 17th century the decoration, particularly of the bow and stern of large ships, became like contemporary decoration of houses and furniture, very rich and elaborate.
Frans Halsmuseum Haarlem, Holland.

Hendrick Dubbels (1621-1676, Dutch)
A Dutch Yacht and Other Vessels Becalmed
Near the Shore
(*oil on canvas, 19" x 18-15/16"*)
*The increasing realism of Dutch painting in the 17th
century meant not only more accurate and detailed
pictures of ships but wonderful evocations of the
different moods of the sea, from serenity and calm to
the violence of storm and battle.*
*Reproduced by courtesy of the Trustees, The National
Gallery, London.*

Sir Peter Lely (1618-80, English)
Peter Pett with the "Sovereign of the Seas"
(*Oil painting on canvas, 55" x 61½"*)
*Peter Pett came of a family of shipwrights and
designers. This is symbolized in the picture by the
dividers he holds in his right hand. Behind him is
the stern of his famous "three-decker" of over 400
tons built in 1637.*
National Maritime Museum, Greenwich.

Model

H.M.S. "Prince," 1670

After the Restoration of Charles II in 1660, the English Navy was reorganized and several circumstances occurred which make it possible for us to have a clear and accurate idea of the design, rigging and decoration of late 17th century warships. Two meticulously realistic Dutch painters, Willem van de Velde I and his son Willem the II were appointed marine painters to the King and made many accurate drawings and paintings of ships.

Through a fortunate piece of patronage Samuel Pepys was appointed Secretary to the Admiralty and as a result of his passion for collecting documents, designs, and working drawings, the wonderful naval archive now in the Library of Magdalen College, Cambridge, was amassed.

A further circumstance which allows us to have a clear idea of ship design in these times is the decision of the Admiralty to have a model made of every warship made, before the design was accepted. A number of these contemporary models have survived. This model of the 100-gun flagship of the English fleet is one of them.

A large ship of 1463 tons, she had a crew of 750 men when she was flagship of the Duke of York at the Battle of Solebay. In contrast with Elizabethan ships the upper works fore and aft have been reduced, so that the "Prince" has graceful flowing lines running from bow to stern. To carry the larger guns of Stuart times, hulls were designed to be wider at the water line and to slope in towards the top deck. The largest guns were placed nearest the water line. Three masts were used instead of the earlier four and a strangely insecure looking addition, a sprit-sail topmast, was fitted at the end of a short bowsprit. This latter was to be replaced in the next century by a staysail under the bowsprit and jibs above.
British Crown Copyright, Science Museum London.

Detail
Bow and Figurehead from the "Prince."
This shows the richness of carving on the bow and also the shorter upward curving breakhead which ends in the equestrian figurehead, and which is much shorter than in Elizabethan times.
British Crown Copyright, Science Museum London.

Abraham Storck (1644-c. 1705, Dutch)
The Four Day Fight
(1666, oil painting, 31″ x 43½″)
National Maritime Museum, Greenwich.

Model
H.M.S. "Boyne," 80 guns
(*1692*)
This contemporary model shows the arrangement of the decks. Below the water line the model has not been planked and you can see how the ribs are fitted into the keel. All these large ships are carvel built with the planks fitted edge to edge. The gaps between were caulked with a mixture of tar, hair, sulphur and tallow which was also painted on the surface of the hull to protect the timbers from barnacles and sea worms.
National Maritime Museum, Greenwich.

Drawing

Shipbuilding at Toulon

(c. 1690, pen and ink)

One of 34 drawings in a manuscript, this one shows how French ship design was greatly improved under Louis XIV's minister, Colbert. Dockyards became more efficient and some prefabrication of parts was done to make building quicker. Though at the beginning of the 18th century English shipwrights seem to have thought the French ships were not sufficiently seaworthy, by the end of the century ships captured from the French were used as models for new types of English ships.

National Maritime Museum, Greenwich.

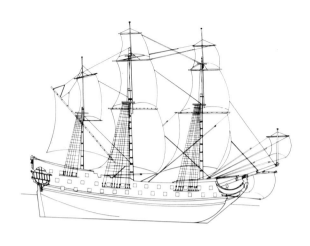

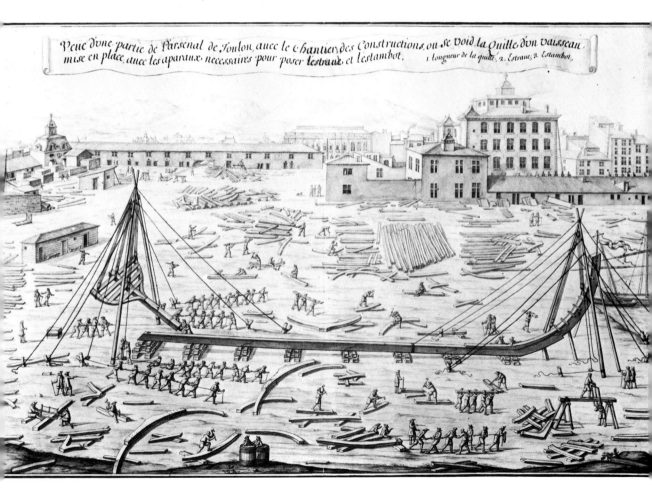

Veue d'une partie de l'arsenal de Toulon, auec le Chantier des Constructions, ou se void la Quille d'un vaisseau mise en place, auec les aparaux necessaires pour poser l'estrave, et l'estambot. 1 longueur de la quille, 2. Estraue, 3. Estambot.

Willem van de Velde the Younger (1633-1707,
Dutch)
The Gust of Wind
(*Oil on canvas, 30½" x 25"*)
Rijksmuseum, Amsterdam.

Willem van de Velde the Younger (1633-1707,
Dutch)
The "Ij" before Amsterdam
(*1688, oil painting, 45¼" x 81"*)
Rijksmuseum, Amsterdam.

Model
H.M.S. "Britannia," 100 guns
(1719)
This model separated at the water line shows several interesting details of construction and design. Below the water the ship is streamlined and graceful, while above, the "Britannia" has the characteristic bulging hull needed to stabilize the three decks of cannon. The four bollard-like projections from the lower gun deck near the bows are the riding bitts to which the anchor cables were attached.
National Maritime Museum, Greenwich.

Model
A 50-Gun Ship
(c. 1736)
*As well as showing a stage in the gradual develop-
ment of the hull through the 17th and 18th
centuries, this 18th–century model gives a very
detailed idea of the rigging of a three-master. The
"Gloucester" was part of the squadron with which
Anson sailed to circumnavigate the world in 1740.
However, she was badly damaged during a storm
in 1742 and was sunk at Anson's orders.
British Crown Copyright, Science Museum, London.*

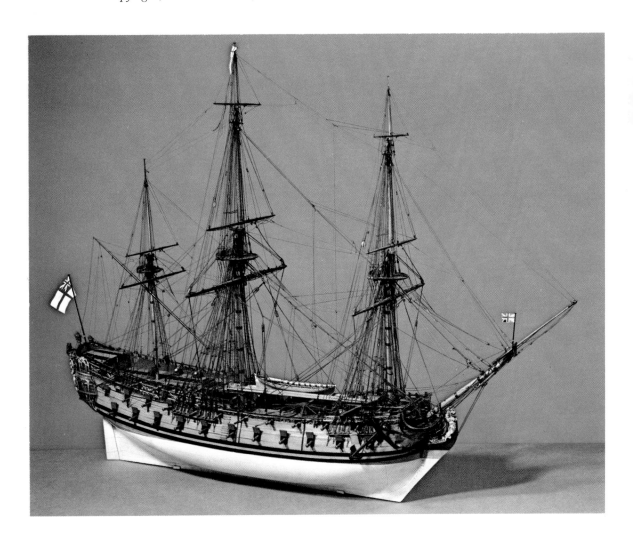

John Hood (*fl. 1750-70, English*)
The Indiaman "Falmouth"
(*1752, a section and plan*)
Except for their larger holds, merchant ships were not very different in design from warships and most of them carried cannon. The "Falmouth" had 34 gun ports, mostly on the main deck. In the section drawing you can see that the waist, the space between the fo'c'sle and the poop, is decked over except for a grating in the centre section. Aft of the foremast on the main deck is the galley stove. Amidships is the main capstan for raising the anchors (most ships at this time carried at least four). There is a second capstan on the poop deck between the main and mizzen masts. Passengers were carried in the poop and on the main deck aft.
National Maritime Museum, Greenwich.

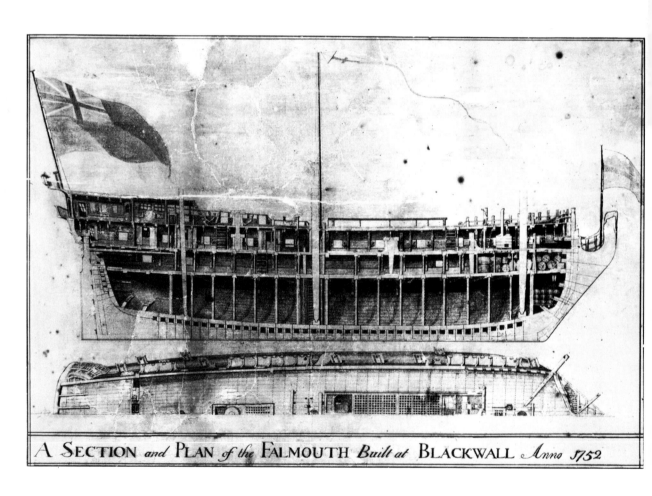

A SECTION and PLAN of the FALMOUTH Built at BLACKWALL Anno 1752

John Clevely the Elder (c. 1745-1786, English)
A Sixth-Rate on the Stocks
(1758, Oil painting, 26½" x 51")
This and other paintings by Clevely are interesting because they show the Naval dockyards at Deptford and give some idea of how ships were built and maintained in the 18th century. In this painting a small 25 gun ship is on the stocks and ready for launching and another small ship is in dry dock being repaired and re-rigged. Small warships of this kind were used against French privateers.
National Maritime Museum, Greenwich.

After Willem van de Velde the Elder
Two English Third Rates in a Squall
(*c. 1675, oil painting, 30½" x 66"*)
National Maritime Museum, Greenwich.

Model
Capt. Cook's H.M.S. "Endeavour"
(1768)

Capt. Cook before he joined the Navy had been an officer in ships of this kind carrying coal down the east coast of England. When he was preparing for his first voyage of exploration into the Pacific he chose this ship. Built as a merchant ship at Whitby in 1764 and originally named the "Earl of Pembroke", she was bought by the Admiralty and renamed the "Endeavour." Slow sailing and sturdy, she was almost the same size as Columbus's "Santa Maria." Her broad build meant that she could be safely and easily beached for periodic scraping of the hull.
National Maritime Museum, Greenwich.

previous page:
John Clevely the Elder (c. 1745-1786, English)
"Royal George" off Depford
(1757, oil painting, 48" x 74")
The picture shows the Thames at Deptford crowded with small boats, including a Dutch barge, that have come to watch the launching of a large warship.
National Maritime Museum, Greenwich.

Model
"Royal George," 100 guns
(1756)
National Maritime Museum, Greenwich.

John Hood (active 1762-71, English)
The Hudson's Bay Company's Fleet ("Prince Rupert," "Sea Horse" and "King George") leaving Gravesend for Hudson Bay
(1769, wash drawing, 25½" x 49½")
Courtesy of the Hudson's Bay Company, London.

J. M. W. Turner (1775-1851, English)
Calais Pier
(1803, oil painting, 67¾" x 94½")
This painting by Turner shows the English cross-channel packet (the crowded boat with the brown sails) arriving at Calais on a stormy day while various fishing boats manoeuvre in the mouth of the harbour. Great numbers of these small, very sturdy boats with single masts and simple sail arrangements were used through the 17th, 18th and 19th centuries for fishing and trading. They often worked from coasts where there were no harbours, landing on beaches to put down and collect their cargoes; yet many survived for more than 50 years, a comment on the skill and knowledge of local waters of their captains!
Reproduced by courtesy of the Trustees, The National Gallery, London

George Arnald (1763-1841, English)
The Destruction of the "Orient," 1 August
1798
(Oil painting, 73" x 106")
This painting, like others that record Nelson's battles
may not be as good as those by the 17th century
Dutch painters, but it is certainly dramatic. It
shows the explosion that occurred after the French
flagship had caught fire during the Battle of the Nile.
National Maritime Museum, Greenwich Hospital
Collection.

J. M. W. Turner (1775-1851, English)
Sketch of a Wreck
(c. 1805, Pen, ink and wash)
This small sketch catches perhaps more dramatically
than many larger pictures the terror of a wreck at
sea. It also has some poignancy in relation to the
"Peter and Sarah" which was lost in the great gale
of 1859 on the North Devon coast.
British Museum, London.

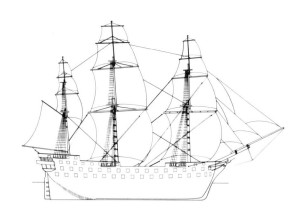

Photograph

The ship "Peter and Sarah," built 1809

This old photograph, probably taken in 1859, shows a small 50-foot two-master similar to many ships that brought immigrants to North America. Mr. Gillis writes: "In September 1818 the "Peter and Sarah" sailed from Bideford to Richmond Bay, Prince Edward Island, carrying two trained shipwrights, several journeymen and apprentices who were to build a 200-ton fully rigged ship. They were to clear a patch of forest and erect a cabin to live in through the severe winter!"

Photograph courtesy of Richard Gillis Collection, Newquay, Cornwall, U.K.

Model
H.M.S. "Constance," 50 guns
(1846)
The "Constance" was converted to a steamship in 1862 and can therefore be thought of as both the climax of the design of sailing warships and as its termination. The fore and aft castles of medieval ships, traces of which remain in hull design until the 18th century, have gone and an unbroken main deck runs from bowsprit to stern. Perhaps the most obvious change in rig is in the number of sails carried on the mizzenmast. There are four square sails and the older lateen has been replaced by a gaff sail held down by a boom which sticks out over the stern. This sail was called a "driver" or a "spanker."
National Maritime Museum, Greenwich.

W. J. Huggins (1781-1845, English)
East Indiaman "Edinburgh" entering the Strait of Sunda
(Oil painting on canvas, 30" x 40")
Collection: Art Gallery of Hamilton, Ontario. Gift of Mrs. Julius Griffith, 1958.

J. H. Wright
U.S. Ship "Constellation"
(1833, oil painting on canvas, 20" x 30")
During the 19th century there were a number of artists who specialized in painting ship portraits for owners or captains. Often seamen, particularly the ship's carpenter, also painted or even embroidered pictures of ships or scenes at sea.
Courtesy; Museum of Fine Arts, Boston, M. and M. Karolik Collection.

James E. Butterworth (1817-94)
Clipper Ship "Great Republic"
(*1853, oil painting on canvas, 17¾" x 23⅜"*)
By 1838 when the first steamship service across the Atlantic had been inaugurated, merchant sailing ships were threatened by steam. However, partly as a result of improved design, partly because they were cheaper and more reliable, many sailing ships, both large and small, were used until 1900.

From the 1840's onwards the New England shipbuilders established a reputation for fast three-masted clippers. These provided the fastest passage around the Horn in the California gold rush 1847, and the later Australian gold rush, and their success led to their design being copied in Europe. Most clipper ships were three-masted, ranging from 750 to 1800 tons. The "Great Republic" was the first 19th-century four-master, though in the 1880's many four-masters with steel hulls and up to 3000 tons burden were built for the Australian wool and wheat trade.

The Peabody Museum, Salem, Massachusetts. Photo by M. W. Sexton.

CLIPPER SHIP DREADNOUGHT OFF TUSKAR LIGHT

After a painting by D. MacFarlane
Clipper Ship "Dreadnought" off Tuskar Light
(*1856, Lithograph, 16" x 24⅜", published by*
N. Currier)
Courtesy: The Mariners Museum, Newport News,
Virginia.

English wood engraving
Ship Under Sail
(*c. 1800*)
Dover Publications.

Commemorative Postage Stamp (*Canadian*)
The "Bluenose"
(*Engraving, issued 1929*)

Because of the skill of local shipwrights and the good timber available, the 19th-century Maritimes shipyards produced many fast sailing ships. The "Bluenose" was one of the most celebrated of the Lunenburg schooners, designed for fishimg on the Grand Banks. These schooners achieved their fame in the International Fishermen's Trophy Races of 1920-38.

Courtesy of George S. Wegg.

English wood engraving
A Naval Engagement
(*c. 1800*)
Dover Publications.

THE MARINERS MIRROVR

Wherin may playnly be seen the courses, heights, distances, depths, soundings, flouds and ebs, risings of lands, rocks, sands and shoalds, with the marks for th'entrings of the Harbouroughs, Havens and Ports of the greatest part of Europe: their seueral traficks and commodities: Together w.th the Rules and instrumēts of NAVIGATION.

First made & set fourth in diuers exact Sea-Charts, by that famous Nauigator *LVKE WAGENAR of Enchuisen.* And now fitted with necessarie additions for the use of Englishmen by ANTHONY ASHLEY.

Herein alsf may be vnderstood the exploits lately atchieued by the right Honorable the L. Admerall of England with her Ma.ties Nauie and some former seruices don by that worthy Knight S.r FRA: DRAKE.

Nautical Equipment

The emphasis on efficiency in design is characteristic of most of the equipment that sailors used, especially of their nautical maps and instruments. These had to be simple and easy to read, but they were also handsome and sturdy pieces of workmanship.

The ancient sailors had very few, if any, navigational instruments or maps. They navigated by the stars and by landmarks and currents that they had memorized. To the sailors of the harsh North Atlantic, the stormy and often fog-bound coastline was a paradox: it was dangerous to get too close, but it was also dangerous to let it out of sight. They sailed from headland to headland; when a headland was sighted, from as far out to sea as possible, a course was set for the next headland.

A sailor who sails his ship within sight of land by knowing landmarks, shoals, currents and tides, is called a pilot. In the later Middle Ages such seamen were usually illiterate and had to learn gradually by heart the characteristics of the coasts they navigated, for they had no charts or instruments other than a *compass* and a *lead and line*. Invented in China, a compass made it possible, when the sun or stars

"The Mariner's Mirrour."
Title Page
(1588, engraving 13" x 9¾")
This is an English translation of Waghenaer's "Spieghel der Zeevaerdt." It shows the instruments of the navigator, the terrestial and heavenly globes, the sand glass, quadrant, astrolabe and cross-staff, lead and line, dividers and compass.
British Museum, London.

could not be seen, to set a course from headland to headland. The lead and line, a weighted rope measured off in fathoms, allowed the sailor to measure how much water was under the keel of his ship, and to know where he was from the smell or colour of the mud or sand that stuck to tallow smeared on the bottom of the lead.

Later, sailors realized that one of the advantages of being able to read and write was that they could keep a written record of the coastal characteristics. At the end of the fifteenth century and during the sixteenth century several of these pilot notebooks were published as printed *rutters* or route-books. These rutters contained not only written descriptions of landmarks but also information about the tides. Tides along the coast of Northern Europe were very important to sailors, for they produced strong changes of current and occurred at different times each day and in different places along a stretch of coastline. It was important for a sailor to know not only where he was going but also how high the tide would be when he got there. For example, along part of the east coast of England the spring tide rises more than twenty-one feet, so that at low tide a ship could be wrecked on rocks which she could safely sail over at high water.

Sailing has always been a dangerous business. Anthony Ashley's "Exhortation to the Apprentices of the Art of Navigation," printed in the *Mariner's Mirrour* of 1588, was advice to be taken seriously by anyone who did not wish to drown.

"The first and chiefest way to attayne to the perfect skill and science of Navigation is whensoever any Shipmaster or Mariner shall set forth from land out of any River or Hauven, diligently to marke what buildings, Castles, Towers, Churches, Hils, Bals, Dounes, Windmils or other marks are standing on the land. All which, or many of them let him pourtray with his penne, how they beare and how farre distaunt: but uppon the true and certeine poynts of the Compasse, uppon which hee first set sayle, and shaped his course, whilst yet every mark on the land may bee clearly and evidently perceaved, to the end that true arising there of may be the better had. He must also very often cast the Lead that he may most exactly note in his compte-booke, how farre off, all the Shoalds and sands lie from the Shoare."

Most rutters had only written descriptions of the coastline. However, in 1520, Pierre Gracie published *Le Grant Routtier* and included some simple but remarkably vigorous woodcuts of the outlines of various capes and headlands. His idea was to give the distinctive silhouette of headlands, almost to caricature them, so that a seaman catching a glimpse of a landfall in bad weather would be able to recognize it and know where he might sail in safety.

Once sailors became more adventurous and went out of sight of land they had to know other ways of getting from place to place. They needed accurate charts showing enlarged, detailed sections of maps. Knowledge of the shape and distribution of the continents gradually developed from that of classical times through information gleaned from the journeys of the great maritime explorers. This knowledge made possible the growing accuracy of maps.

At first, the charts provided the sailor with only an outline of the coast and with compass bearings and distances between various places. Gradually they included very important information about the kinds of shoreline, the depth of the water and location of rocks or sandbars.

These early maps show an increasingly more precise realization of the shape and detail of the continents. But above all they are beautiful in their design, colouring, special ornamental *cartouches* and lettering. The older maps frequently have illustrations in the margins showing views of harbours, figures of the native peoples, whales or strange monsters, ships in full sail or elaborate compass roses. These maps were unique pen drawn manuscripts with water colour added.

As the demand for maps and charts increased, they were reproduced by printing. Some of the earliest were printed from woodcut blocks. After 1550, maps and charts were usually engraved onto copper plates from which large editions could be printed, the colour being added by hand. A tradition of map design, using the clear firm line that the burin* makes in copper, developed and continued through the sixteenth, seventeenth, and eighteenth centuries. It is fascinating to see how a particular technique, such as engraving in copper affects the character of the maps it is used to create. It is also interesting to compare the similarities in the kinds of ornaments used by map-makers and shipbuilders in a particular period. The style of ornamentation and design at any given time is surprisingly consistent; shapes of a similar character occur whether they are in a chair, a woman's shoe, the stern of a ship or a *cartouche* on a map.

A development in the art of navigation occurred with the deep-sea sailor, who sailed over great stretches of sea without landmarks. In order to travel safely from place to place he needed not only detailed and accurate maps and charts but also new and complicated navigational instruments. He could tell how well he was progressing only if he knew his speed and direction. During the fifteenth and sixteenth centuries, a log, a flanged board attached to a rope measured off with knots at regular intervals, was thrown over the stern and the speed at which the knots ran out was timed with a small sandglass. This way of estimating speed was not very accurate; sailors such as Columbus usually overestimated how fast they were going. Without landmarks, it was difficult to be sure about the direction in which a ship was sailing; in this uncertain situation the sailor periodically needed to be able to fix his position. He could do this if he knew how far north or south (latitude), east or west (longitude) he was of his starting point. It proved to be easier to find the latitude than the longitude. The sailor could find out how far north or south he was if he measured the height of the sun or certain stars above the horizon. He was helped by mathematicians, who provided the tables of latitude, and by the astronomers, who developed simplified versions of the instruments used to measure angles of elevation of heavenly bodies: the *cross staff, astrolabe* and *quadrant*. As knowledge increased and design improved, these instruments became more accurate.

The Portuguese kings, John II and Manuel, were the first to realize the importance of navigation to exploration and trade, founding schools where captains could learn how to use the new scientific instruments. Like most such

*For description of copper engraving see *The Artist's Workshop*, pp. 57-65.

instruments which must be simple and efficient, they have, like the ships themselves, a high standard of craftsmanship and a purposeful beauty of shape and arrangement.

The medieval merchant seaman sailing the Atlantic seaboard, and the Portuguese seaman exploring the west coast of Africa, were not greatly concerned about longitude because they were not sailing great distances to the east or west. But after Columbus had crossed the Atlantic and Vasco De Gama had entered the Indian Ocean, it became increasingly important to be able to calculate longitude accurately. Many ships were wrecked and many men died through the lack of this knowledge. For example, in 1741 eighty crewmen died of scurvy on board "Centurion" because Captain Anson could not establish the longitude of his landfall on the coast of Chile. The easiest way of doing this was by knowing the time, but not until the middle of the eighteenth century did anyone make a clock that could keep time accurately at sea.

In 1714 the British Government established the Board of Longitude, which offered a prize of £20,000 to anyone who could consistently calculate longitude to within thirty miles after a voyage of six weeks. This prize was won in 1773 by a Yorkshire carpenter named John Harrison, who finally produced the winning watch (a little over five inches in diameter) only after he had built three much larger timepieces. It took him 17 years to build timepiece Number 3. The difficulty was to make a clock that would keep very accurate time in spite of temperature changes and the violent movement of a ship in rough weather. At that time no one on the Board of Longitude believed that this was possible. Only after Captain Cook took a copy of Harrison's Number 4 watch with him on his second and third Pacific voyages was Harrison's amazing achievement finally recognized.

Juan de la Cosa
Columbus' Discoveries in the New World
(*Large Portolan Chart, drawn 1500*)
The illustration is a reproduction of a manuscript map in the Naval Museum in Madrid that was drawn by Juan de la Cosa, who sailed with Columbus.
Map Division, The New York Public Library, Astor Lennox and Tilden Foundations.

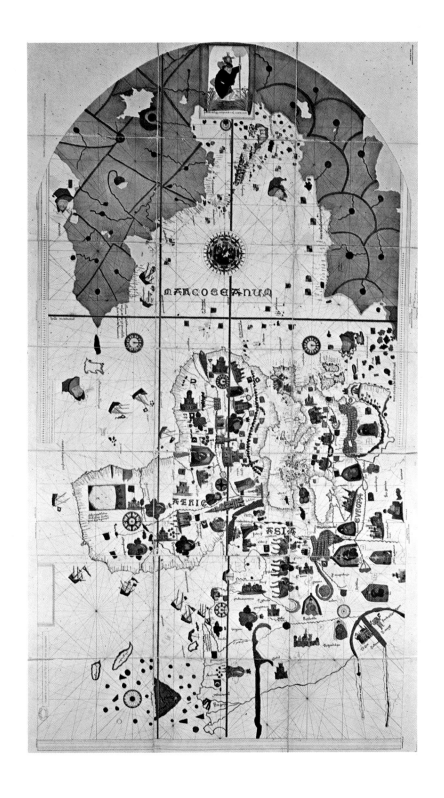

73

Sache que deuãt vermeo ya vne isle qui se nomme lisle de essayrault Et se monstre tel.

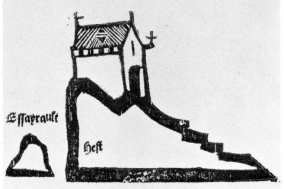

Sache que quant tu seras aual de maschessac il te aparoistra ditelle maniere Mais quant tu seras en amont il se mõstre estre plus ront et plus hault du bout damont.

Pour bien congnoistre Lissedieu si est que tu voyras aussi tost ou plustost le clochier de se glise que la terre de belle veue

Lissedieu gist est et noroest et est semblable a ceste figure.

Sy tu va se bas pour querir se pillier Et veille ranger de vers noirmonster pour toy garder des dangiers deuers noirmonstier il fault que tu aye la tour de noirmõstier la haulteur dung homme au dessus de troys gros puysde sable qui sont de uers la mer et aussi sont les plus bas et les plus haultz.

Et quant tu seras en bon chenal tu trouueras douze brasses a quatorze brasses deaue.

Et si se vent est damont et tu veulx ranger pres ne va point plus pres de six brasses si tu ne scay bien commẽt car quant tu seras a six brasses si tu cours sus se nort ou sus se nort noroest

Woodcuts
"Le Grant Routtier et Pyllotage et Encrage de la Mer", Second edition, 1521.
Woodcuts of "Isla Izaro" and "Cabo Machichaco," and of "Les Chiens Perrins and Punta du Butte."
Source: "Rutters of the Sea" by D. W. Waters, Yale University Press; Beinecke Libary, Yale University, Henry C. Taylor Collection.

Vallard's Atlas 1546
Map of Canada
Detail: Cartier Landing with Colonists in 1541.
(13" x 17")
*Here you have the strange inconsistency of a map
with scenes of colonists and Indians in a landscape
painted within the outline of the coast.*
British Museum, London.

following page:
Henricus Martellus Germanus
World Map
(1489)
*This manuscript map shows the world as it was
thought of before Columbus sailed westward. Asia
is based on the ancient descriptions of Ptolemy and
those of Marco Polo. Africa is accurate and detailed
for those parts explored by Dias in 1487.*
British Museum, London.

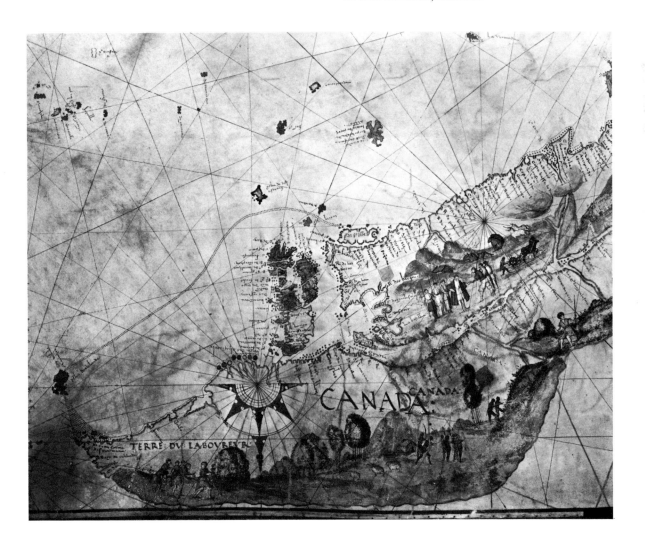

John Huighen Van Linschoten
Map of the South Atlantic (Oceanus Aethiopicus)
From van Linschoten's "Itinerario" printed at Amsterdam, 1596. London, 1598.
National Maritime Museum, Greenwich.

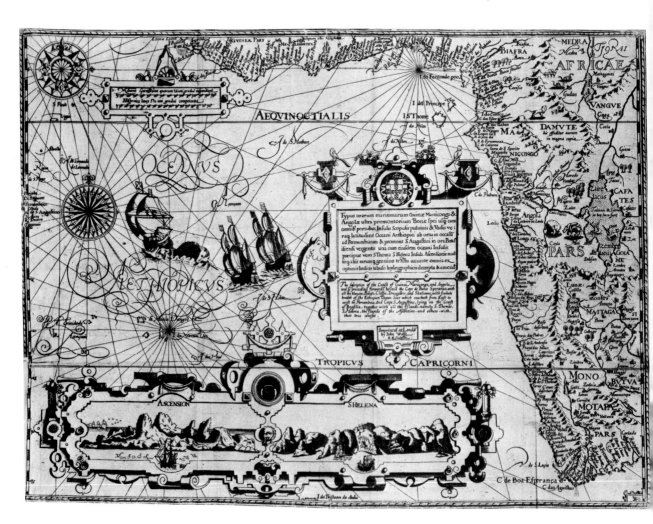

Gerard Mercator (1512-94)
Double Cordiform Map of the World
(*Engraving, published at Lourain in 1538, 13" x 20½"*)

All maps existed in manuscript form, but once interest in maps increased they were printed, sometimes from woodcuts, but more usually from copper engravings which gave a particularly clear and and precise outline. The way a map was reproduced affected its design and the forms that decoraction and lettering took. The flowing italic lettering on this map is particularly handsome.

These world maps to some extent inspired the early navigators and determined their idea of the placing of the continents. Their discoveries in turn reshaped the maps. One of the inaccuracies of a map is that it is flat and the earth's surface is not. Over short distances this may not be important, but on a long voyage it may be critical. Mercator's map is an attempt to project this curved surface onto the page in such a way that the distances will not be too inaccurate.
British Museum, London.

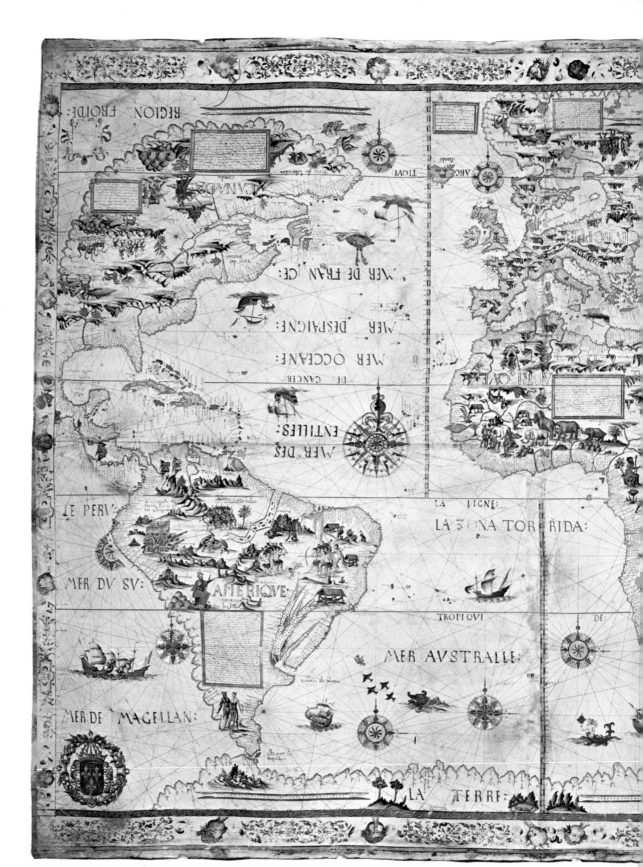

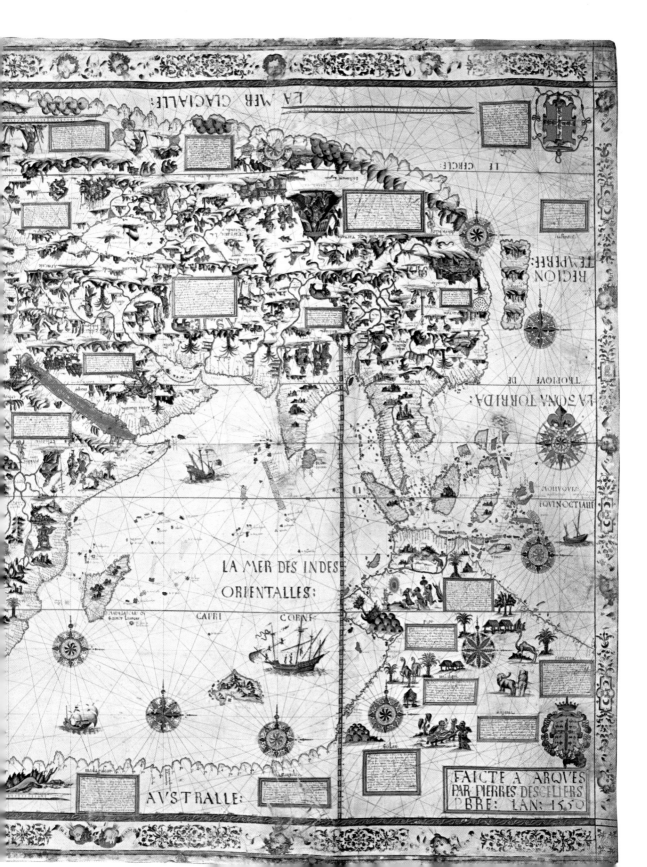

previous page:
Pierre Desceliers
World Map
(1550)
Desceliers was a priest from Calais who probably produced this large manuscript map for Henry II of France. It was intended to be looked at on a table so that the lettering reads both up and down.
British Museum, London.

Willem Blaeuw (1571-1638)
World Map
(From Blaeuw's "Toanneet des Aerdrycx Neiuwe Atlas, Printed in Amsterdam, 1635.)
This very handsome map is ornamented with pictures of the planets, the elements, the seasons and the seven wonders of the world. The engraved outline and the decoration has been emphasized with water colour. It would be hard to claim that this is any more utilitarian than the carved and richly ornamented sterns of warships being built at this time.
British Museum, London.

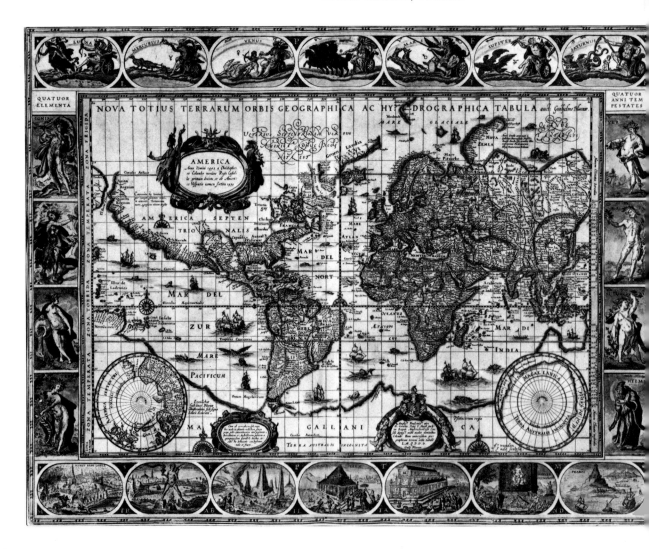

Brass Astrolabe

This instrument was found in 1867 and is probably that lost by Champlain on his journey up the Ottawa River in 1613. The astrolabe is a simplified version of astronomers' instruments. It consisted of a circular disk suspended from a ring and a rotatable crossbar with sights, the "alidade." To use the astrolabe it was suspended by its ring and the desired star was sighted along the alidade (not always easy on the moving deck of a ship).
Public Archives of Canada, Ottawa.

Renaissance Sea Compass

The most primitive compass was a needle, magnetized from a lodestone and floating on a wood chip in a bowl of water. The compass illustrated here consists of a circular card balanced on a pin and with a piece of magnetized wire glued to the undersurface. The card or fly was marked with the four principal winds and a total of either 32 or 64 points.

The early compasses seem to have been housed in chests containing a lamp. These chests are forerunners of the binnacle which protected the compass and made it possible to read it at night.
National Maritime Museum, Greenwich.

83

Humphrey Cole of London
Nocturnal
(*c. 1580*)
A nocturnal was used to tell the time at night. The small pointer marked with a sun was set for the day (in this case August 15). The Pole Star was sighted through the central hole and the pointer was lined up with Kochab, the brightest of the "guards," the stars that rotate around the Pole Star. It would seem to be about 12.40 A.M.!
British Museum, London.

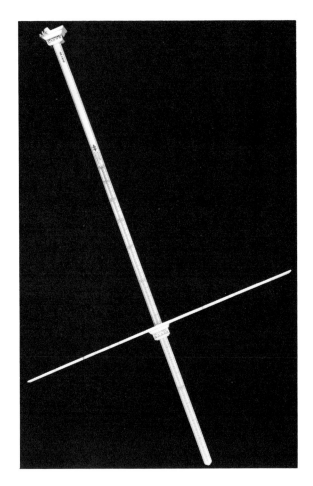

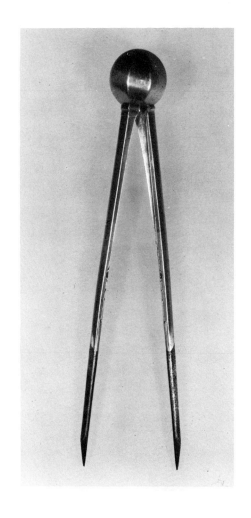

Thomas Tuttell of Charing Cross
Cross-staff
(London c. 1695)
The cross-staff consisted of a rod, usually of box-wood, about three feet long and ¾" in section on which a cross piece could slide. The cross piece was moved along the rod until it measured the distance from the star to the horizon when the tip of the rod was held to the eye. A reading in degrees could then be taken from the scale on the rod. Its disadvantage was that it could only be used at dawn or dusk when both the stars and the horizon were visible.
National Maritime Museum, Greenwich.

17th-century brass dividers
An elegant instrument used to measure off distances on a chart.
National Maritime Museum, Greenwich.

18th-Century Sextant

This instrument was invented by John Hadley in 1713. It was a development from the primitive quadrant, which you see illustrated near the top of the title page of the "Mariner's Mirrour," which was an inaccurate instrument, difficult to use. The sextant (a sixth rather than a quarter of a circle) aligned light from the star and from the horizon by means of a telescopic sight and supplied a reading on a Vernier scale.

National Maritime Museum, Greenwich.

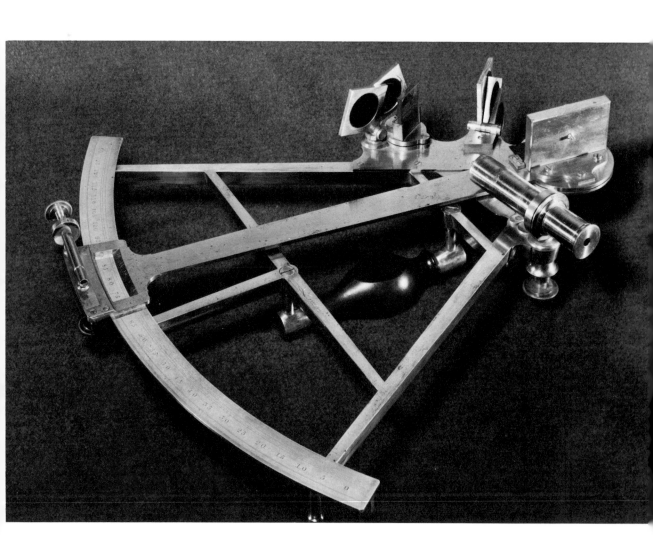

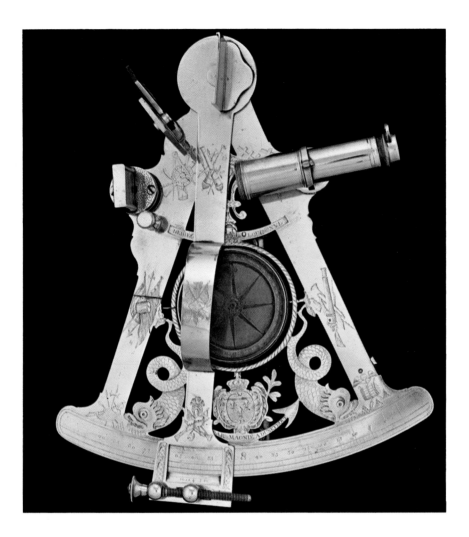

Magnie of Dunkerque
Brass sextant
(*c. 1786*).
Both of the sextants illustrated here are characteristic of the handsome workmanship found in navigational instruments of the 18th century.
Courtesy: The Peabody Museum of Salem.
Photo by M. W. Sexton.

John Harrison
No. 1 Marine Timekeeper
(1735)
In the early part of the 18th century no one believed
that it was possible to make a clock that would
keep accurate time on a rolling ship in damp air and
with frequent changes of temperature. John Harrison,
who previously had no experience at clock making,
worked for six years to produce this first chronometer.
The first three clocks that he designed were large
by contrast; the fourth chronometer is only 5.2"
diameter, little bigger than a large watch.
National Maritime Museum, Greenwich.

following page:
John Harrison
No. 4 Timekeeper: Backplate
(1757)
Looking at this illustration it is easy to recognize the
justice of what John Harrison himself proudly wrote
of his watch: "I think I may make so bold as to say,
that there is neither any other Mechanical or
Mathematical thing in the world that is more
beautiful or curious in texture than this my watch or
timekeeper for the Longitude."
National Maritime Museum, Greenwich, on loan
from Ministry of Defence, Navy.

The study of sailing ships and instruments fosters an understanding of their gradual development and an appreciation for their increasingly ingenious adaptation to the work they are intended to do. However, even when compelled to admire their wonderful craftsmanship, it may be difficult to be certain that there is any necessary relation between the design of useful things and their beauty. Nonetheless when I look at the back plate of Harrison's Number 4 timekeeper, I can understand the old man's pride in this wonderful object, which, like many other things illustrated in this book, seems to suggest that there is a dignity in utilitarian things, and in the honest and unpretentious craftsmanship of their makers, which gives them a worth, even a quality of goodness, which can properly be called beauty.

GLOSSARY

across the wind—A ship sails "across the wind" when the wind is blowing on the port or starboard quarter, that is on the left or right side.

aft—The stern (rear) of a ship as opposed to the fore (front) or bow at the opposite end.

astrolabe—A simplified version of astronomers' instruments. It consisted of a circular disk suspended from a ring and a rotatable crossbar with sights: the alidade. To use the astrolabe, it was suspended by its ring and the desired star was sighted along the alidade.

before the wind—A ship is sailing "before the wind" when the wind is blowing from the rear.

boom—A pole that pivots on the mast and is attached to the bottom of a sail.

bowsprit—A fixed pole that projects forward from the bow.

broadsides—In most sailing ships few guns fired over the bow (front) or stern (rear). Most were arranged along the sides. Though these could be fired singly they were most effective when used as a "broadside;" that is, when all the guns on one side were fired simultaneously.

burden—The capacity of a ship usually measured in tons. Capacity was measured in many ways but for English ships it seems to have been the number of "tonneau" of casks of Bordeaux wine that a ship could carry. A tonneau equalled about 2200 lbs.

cartouche—A sculptured, drawn or painted ornamental frame, frequently oval in shape, around an inscription, monogram, map title or coat of arms.

close to the wind—No ship can sail directly towards the oncoming wind, but when the sails are "close hauled" it is often possible to sail against the wind at an angle of 40 or 50 degrees to the wind direction. The smaller this angle the closer the ship is sailing to the wind.

cross-staff—A cross-staff consisted of a rod, usually made of boxwood, about three feet long and ¾" in diameter on which a cross piece could slide. The cross piece was moved along the rod until it measured the distance from a star to the horizon when the tip of the rod was held to the eye. A reading in degrees could then be taken from the scale on the rod. Its disadvantage was that it could only be used at dawn or dusk when both stars and the horizon were visible.

dhows—Arab sailing ship usually fitted with two lateen sails. Such ships are still used in the Persian Gulf and the Indian Ocean.

draught—The depth of water needed to allow a ship to float, or the distance from the water line to the bottom of the ship. This depth will of course vary with the size of the ship's cargo.

following wind—A following wind is one that is blowing from directly behind a ship.

fore—The bow or front of a ship.

forecastle—fo'c'sle—This originally referred to the structure built over the bow (front). It came to mean the crew's quarters in the raised front part of the ship.

freeboard—The sides of a ship, or the distance from the water line to the top of the side (see "gunwale").

gaff—A pole pivoting on the mast and attached to the top of the sail.

gunports—A series of openings made in the sides of warships through which cannon were fired. These openings were fitted with doors hinged along their top edges and called "scuttles," which could be raised to allow the guns to be aimed and fired and could be closed to prevent water coming in.

gunwale, gunnel—The top edge of a ship's side, so called because it was originally used to support guns.

halyard, halliard—The ropes used to raise and lower the yards and sails. These are called the "running rigging" in contrast to the "standing rigging" which brace the masts into the hull.

into the wind—Since a ship cannot sail directly towards the oncoming wind it sails in that direction (windward) by tacking (see "tacking").

jib—A triangular sail set on a rope running from the bowsprit to the top of the foremast (see "bowsprit").

lateen—A triangular rigged sail set on a pole that is attached to the mast diagonally. It was first developed by the Arabs. In the western world lateen sails were usually set on the rear mast only.

mainstay—The rope bracing the mainmast to the bow or to the front mast. The mainmast is the chief mast of the ship, usually the one second from the front.

mizzenmast—The rear mast on a three- or four-masted ship.

poop—Name given to the rear part of a sailing ship.

privateer—A privately owned ship operating under "letters of marque," which were a licence to attack enemy ships. Drake had such a licence when he attacked the Spanish fleet at Cadiz in 1587. Without letters of marque a privateer becomes a pirate.

quadrant—A primitive instrument used to measure the elevation of a star above the horizon in order to chart a course.

reef points—A series of small ropes attached to both sides of the sail in horizontal rows. By means of these, sections of the sail could be folded and tied up. This is called "reducing sail," either furling a sail altogether or reducing its size so that it catches less wind.

spar—Any pole or beam used to support and spread the sails.

tacking—Sailing in a series of diagonal courses to the right and left in order to move directly against the direction of the prevailing wind.

tiller—Lever or beam by which the rudder is turned.

trim the sails—To raise or turn the sails so that they will catch the wind to the best advantage.

working up wind, working to windward—A ship sailing diagonal courses towards the wind, or tacking, is working up wind. It is often a slow and laborious business, for the sails must be reset after each change of course.

yard (yardarm)—A beam slung across the mast from which a sail is hung. Either end of the yard is called the yardarm.